D1798061

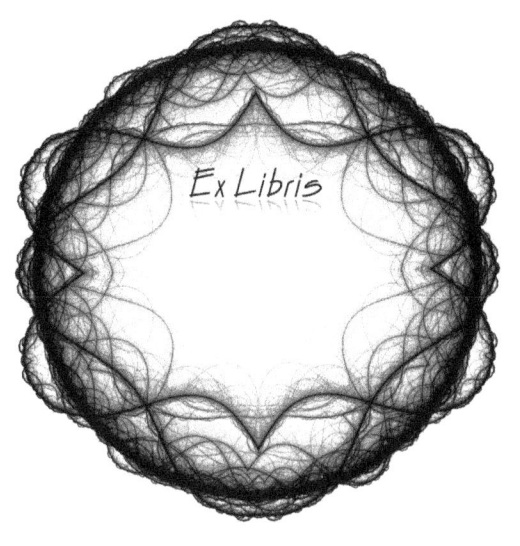

Ex Libris

LETTERS TO MYSELF
JOURNAL

LETTERS TO MYSELF JOURNAL
FIREWORKS

First Printing November 2015
Author Judy Powell
Graphics and journal design by Judy Powell
Print-on-demand publishing by BLURB.com

Contact the authors at _JudyPowellArt@gmail.com_
Buy this journal online at BLURB.com
search LETTERS TO MYSELF JOURNAL

Writing our experiences
helps us to remember
and be enriched again.

Our forever wellspring
is held within these pages.

~ Judy Powell 2015

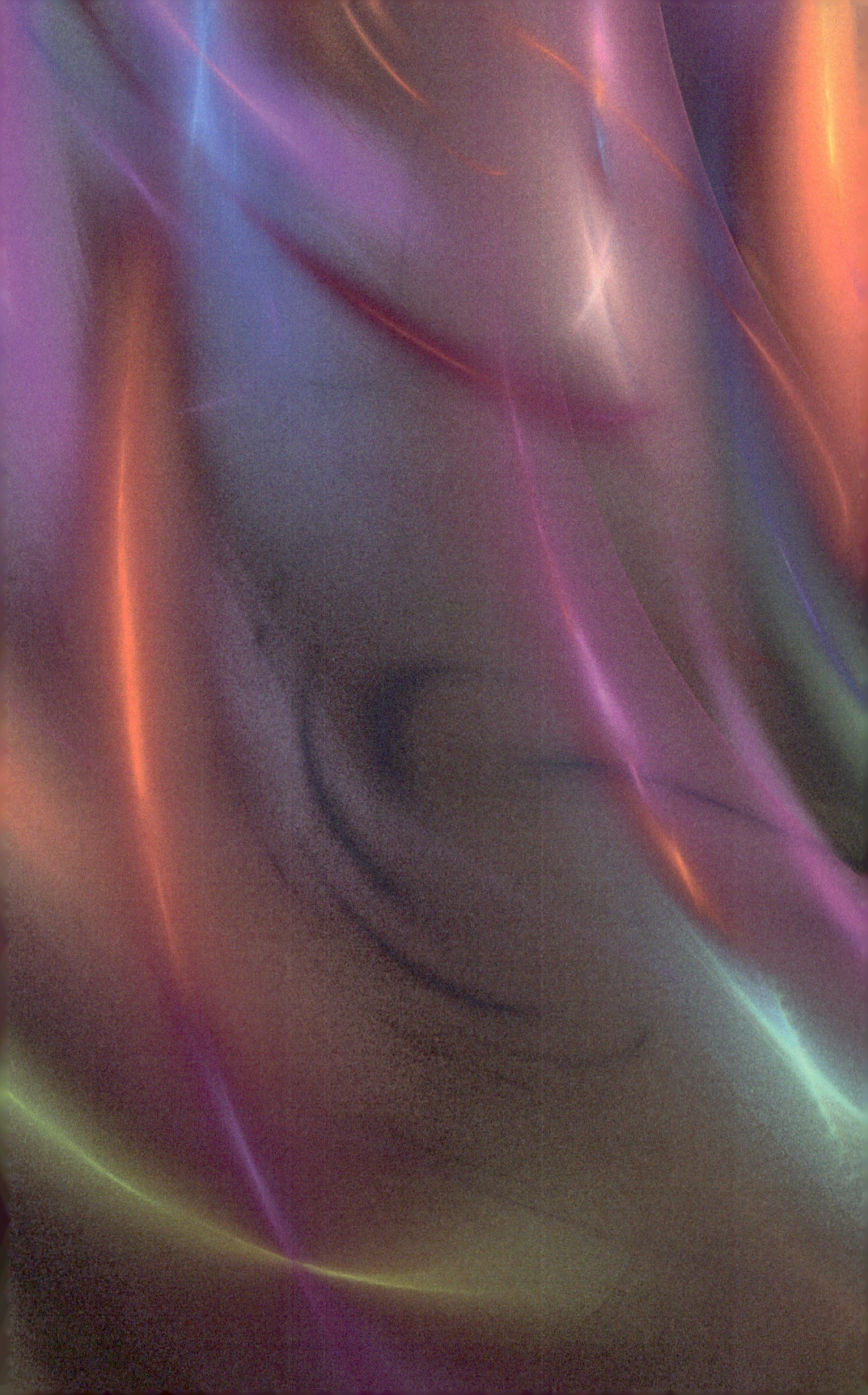

Lightning Source UK Ltd.
Milton Keynes UK
UKHW022258270519
343394UK00001B/9/P